"*One Row After / Bir Sıra Sonra* is a breathtaking interweaving of 'elementary languages in the belly,' and a unique physics which envelop—without restraining—memory, place, relationship, and 'bütün dünya,' the whole world. There is a language here of symbol and space which is built on what is known, but then the author gathers that understanding and takes flight with it, carrying the reader effortlessly, somehow, above. Everything is taken into account, from the alignment of words on the page to the inhale, exhale, and repetition of open spaces. It is, as she writes, a 'locution of atmospheres.'"

—LISA CREECH BLEDSOE
AUTHOR OF *APPALACHIAN GROUND*

"Sonya Wohletz's poems use the sharpest, most purposeful language to build a light-feeling lyric space. This book is a mood to which one may cling. A tremendous reading experience."

—CHRIS GAUMER
MANAGING EDITOR OF *REVOLUTE MAGAZINE*

"How to manage this humanity? Like a (meta)physician or a mystic intoning the good medicine of song, Sonya Wohletz offers in *One Row After / Bir Sıra Sonra* a way of awakening to a world in which all things—animal, vegetable, mineral, and celestial bodies—breathe, probe, thrill, ache, and sigh as we do. Who can feel alone in such a place? To read these poems is to enter a dizzying geography that spans deserts and mountains, south and north, molecule and moon. Wohletz explodes categories, draws and then crosses lines, and allows languages to arise in her verse as they must, from whichever tender root is throbbing to sprout. This way elation lies."

—**D.P. SNYDER**
 TRANSLATOR OF *MEATY PLEASURES*

"Profound yet ethereal, vibrant and emotionally powerful, this multilingual collection is trying, by its complexity, to illuminate the mysteries of the human condition, offering a revelatory meditation on consciousness, memory, language and time. It also reveals the disturbing truth about our own 'voice' which sometimes, distorted, fragmented, fights to stay alive on the page, in spite of the ravaging time. In a highly original style, alternating poetry and prose, the world is 'floating,' parallel voices erupt, or 'our words suspend beyond si | lence,' while 'our feet ... caressed earth in the language of our being.'"

—**STELLA VINITCHI RADULESCU**
 AUTHOR OF *TRAVELING WITH THE GHOSTS*

FIRSTMATTERPRESS

Portland, Ore.

ONE ROW AFTER / BIR SIRA SONRA

ONE ROW AFTER / BIR SIRA SONRA

sonya wohletz

FIRSTMATTERPRESS
Portland, Ore.

First Edition

Published in the United States
by First Matter Press
Portland, Oregon

Paperback ISBN 978-1-958600-04-7

Lead Editors: Lauren Paredes & Caroline Wilcox Reul
Contributing Editors: Ash Good, Natalie Garyet
& Emily Moon

First Matter Press Cohort Collaborators:
Riley Danvers, Xylophone Mykland,
Hailey Spencer & ahuva s. zaslavsky

Cover Illustration: *Hidden Stars* series
Copyright © 2022 by Rachel Mulder
rchlmldr.com

Book design by Ash Good
ashgood.com

FIRSTMATTERPRESS.ORG

*I dedicate these poems to the staff and patients
at Providence St. Peter's Hospital*

*and to Afşin and Çağrı Yılmaz,
my life's greatest blessings.*

POEMS

PART 4   SICAK AYETLER

PART 5   AFTER ALL VERSES ENDING

ENTRY ANGLE

there is a five-pointed star

through   watcher   gaze

frames   entry angle into

verse

our feet   how they   caressed   earth

set forth   call curve

compassion   gently guide

as embrace   gently

the mind of   eternal   and   everything   and

universe   this world   all worlds

united   in

this

there is a five-pointed star

through which the Watcher observes all relation

this   the blue endless   tessellates

                the earth   the path

                                                      called upon

            chorus   balsam

gentle   domain

along   the   pillar(ed)   cavern

in jaw

        reagenting

this wisdom   internal

everything in the universe of this world   of all worlds

united in the veins of

Mother

you entered into this world without veil

at the table   you were seated and   gazed

at the

first half moon   you spoke to us

of terrible things on this earth   I spoke not

our name for there is

no name

you asked for permission

you are blessed

you are blessed

you are blessed

PART 1

PAJARITO

i.

Your hair,   blowing   *through*

hay   hues of afternoon   in   *polaroid,*

the fugitive colors,   bounded   *by season, by station,*

cream, and lighter   *motions of sun,*

and who can agree on the names for   *memory*

in a place like this:

gold, bone, marigold, the evergreen blade, the egg of the sky

shell so fragile as if   we touch   it

as if we turn to flame, to   dust

bleeding toward its edge and the fine crosshatch motions of

pine,   pine,   pine, pry,   and pine

open onto azul, herringboned   *in blue,*

and what else could appear as turquoise stones

along the horizon, along the thin clavicle of the Jemez. There is

a moment, c. 1985,

my brother searching out his hands   *among the aspen*

and he finds himself purchase among lives

that establish themselves   *immensely and*

without shame, though below the surface.

You are pleased as he captures a   *leaf*

large like a gold coin in his   *grasp.*

ii.

He babbles with excitement,

the latest tooth sawing   *through*

and

his tender gums brighten   with   *blood.*

It is hard not to watch you   *instead:*

your eyes are   *dark*

your hair of milfoil   *forests*

in the sculpting waters further north, and

your husband awaits

the seated sky of   this

battle knowledge   *and*

quiet   *weathers.*

iii.

We could have done better, I suppose,

      but it wasn't up for selection that

 morning, whether to place

      the bonnet on the small skull,

or to fold one hand into another

      and pass through the gray gyre

of the mountain, smoothing amidst ridges and swales

      of granite and minute intimations, or

whether the ochre chore of autumn would cede its

      system to the supple urge for

                      further.

1.

Walking through the hallways
socked feet and wet hair,
I come across these
figures

                                        from time to time

They ask questions indirectly,
awaiting an opening,
        an ****

Wanting to see if I'll reaffirm my faith
or establish

                                        communion
                        I always know the answer,
<but when they press further, I break down>

Tongue hammering to glottal stop

I surface/crash

intend/response

and yet

my knowledge of even myself has its animal limits *

*though, that is not to say

this is

a failure

2.

For every question I can't answer,
there is a trajectory

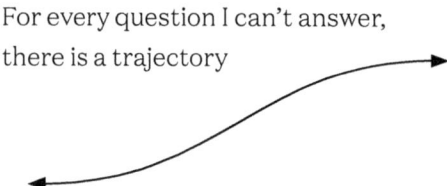

whispered chords admonishing +

thick mosses blooming
their cold compass
across all surfaces

and I am in this way

[sur   r   oun   ded]

by the dense, unyielding arrangement of particles,
frays in the fibers, clusters of calcifications,
and a wandering fever

3.

After a while,

they supply helpfully something along the lines of:

These are the words for mountain in another language

See them gouging into atmospheres?
Alongside, a wreck of turquoise   Before
this, there were the
arrangements
of maps, vehicles, and salt marshes,
small, insipid fish that knew nothing

but
the fogged hope of netting   They swam
in the cistern of stagnate patterns we
                    could've learned to survive

I ask for them, scale by scale,
and refer to the small evidences
along the clay capture   as Mnemosyne

and we
drift forward the re:motioned
haze

4.

When I conclude the skyslide,
they answer: *this is a quarter moon*
and place it in my mouth

There was a marriage on the old school grounds.
The bride wore a blue dress.
The bride was beautiful   her dress, even more beautiful.
Its deep wail and swan,   ascended repose.

Her children from another man
stayed at home with the grandparents.
They cooked and laughed in their relief,
their   hands
clasping air,   the children,   the air.

The wedding guests
a wreck of shrines:
candy on the shelves, hot chocolate, liniments, and tea—
curtains that won't catch fire,   a yardstick at the gate
to measure; or perhaps,   to rupture.

The bride is so alive
and fully realized.
The groom is a shadow,   an idea of a shadow.
The bride is the only thing that is real.
She moves through the maze of this poem,
grace spilling down her spine   a glacier of the last ice age.

Dressed in cold bones and replete with votives,
we mimic language and   crowd
the courses that can't keep   beat
the way the bride does.

Oh, rolling island,
in secret pledge to some middle sea of memory——

What can I courage from a maze besides
the unspooled thread that firmly guides
out from the pit of beasts   to white sails on Monday morning?

I can't kill either.

Or,
more of the same:
the meaning's captured in the grain.

The novice asks: are there other worlds besides the present?
All worlds exist and are united
in the wisdom   of
in the dome   of

A world
Pronounced like sabiduría,
Portraits staged for the evening
                    stethoscope
                        de
                  cada mundo
            of la intercalada
The arrhythmia enmeshed
                        ++   bütün dünya
                    bütün
                    bütün
                    bütün

La sala de espera
Perfumada de anhelos
                        ondan sonra
Las nubes te oían y repentinamente
Te sobró el habla
                        te sobra y te quita
Por eso dijimos,
Ven, y ven   y
                        geleceğiz
                        hoarding fragments in the fists

NaCl or purple potassium, pilloried, abandoned.
Así se asoma
Y se entierran

        <los ángulos del mito, and>

There is the solitude
De un cierto calor
Time expanding the plangent flame
Y no hay nada   mejor que hacer
          (some words left unsaid:
          as in: the trees
          erecting simple skies, or the way
          that the nest opens in flayed
          desire to each new name)
       or rather, the stories
sayillim
Querida sevgilim
Después de 10 años de empeñarse
En la labor de la memoria
What else can unravel
The syllable into the elemental
Melting away of circumstance

PART 2

ROWS, THE SAPPHIRE LIGHT

the early
morning   weaves into itself
morning
images mount   into cloud
and recollect
it silences   speaker

The seed orients the star into five twisting pillars.
They all have numbers,
and we count them, one by one.
They are mostly in order; perhaps
they are not. And the seeds carpet themselves
and are jewels: red, rose, tile, emerald
and spill into the handles of
a leather vessel you wore
on the long journey
across the driest desert
where you learned all the gestures
the birds make when they are
thieving, when they are loving
and when they are lonely.
Stars and vessels, the jewels,
a pillar of planet
spins a neck for itself in prayer
that it might
seed.

La semilla orienta la estrella en cinco pilares torcidos.
Todos tienen sus números
y los contamos, uno por uno.
Y la mayoría están en orden; a lo mejor
no estén. Y las semillas se alfombran
y son joyas: carmín, rosa, azulejo, esmeralda
y éstas se derraman y eran mangas
de la olla de cuero que te llevaste
durante la larga jornada
a través del desierto más seco
donde aprendiste todas las muecas
que hacen los pájaros cuando están robando
cuando están amando,
y cuando están a solas.
Estrellas, ollas y joyas
un pilar de planeta
se teje un cuello en plegaria
que se
semille.

Enunciation:
Do not chase the camera in corner (eye)

though
vision drift
notions its way
in two absconding points of light.
Where they merge
you cannot gaze.

Dismantle and Articulate:
Impossibilities, infirmities.
What remains after the final verse,

And beyond it still
to rest in the darkest chamber.

Rejoinder:

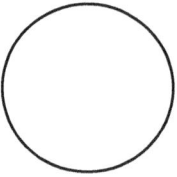

Learn submerge
its steady   pulse

a cool vine
erupts around
the throat of autumn

red leaves mouth open a
crisp rime
across

the fallen
juniper and
smooth dirt

and in that crescive embrace
light pools
a milky opalescence

brims

over

incandescent seed scatters
the swinging
eaves

seeking balance
beneath the stiff ax
of a decelerated sun

chisels a thin
shield

repeats

the promise to bend forward
the ache of time

beyond her

woods mount
in the far corner

and the tender flames
in the gathered fields
rhythm out
the season

snaking sweet sap
into steam of her voice
sloping
faint and familiar

how she called out
extending her hands
when she could not see

into circles of feral dawn
beneath the dream
ledge

glass of water
balanced
there

still

clear geometry of
isosceles stem
flares

pauses

shifting hours

pass through it
like blood

and on the other side
diagonals clear
pressing
flat the
pane

faint
molecules of rust

the departure
of ozone
through hollow
thunder

quickens the cold

thirsts

the golden ground
and sheafs her body
back and forth
in harvest miracle

then
palms close over
in swift
shores

and all the surfaces

slide shut

It's been 4 years and I don't know why I am here again. Buried and clouded in the exhaust that comes with miming a decision that could've been made 50 years ago, or perhaps 5,000. I gaze at my fingers, long and cold as they pull at the green feathers of the verbena plant then crush them in circular gestures. A fragrance erupts a certain solace that I can't comprehend. I pace around this place in search of pens, paper, crayons — nothing extravagant — something ready for the same fingers to grasp. The patients don't realize it, but the doctors walk around each wing, each hallway, each room to bless this place, to bless the patients themselves, every day of every week of every year. Glaciers shift beneath the weight of their knowing. Dust settles on the furniture and is swept away. An owl enters an abandoned shed, and a bright chord in its right brain seeks through layers of dry rot for the warmest place to nest. I want to learn how to hear with my body, to keep pushing beyond the pulsing oracle. And a friend asks if someone can tell him how he got here. It's been months and no one can say. He asks the doctors and nurses every day, and they can't tell him the answer he needs with their voices. And he repeats the story of how his grandfather would gather the children and tell them the story of all creation. He tells us a story of how this grandfather always held his cane in his right hand. How it was, that when he would have need of it, it would appear in his right hand. Beneath the central air he speaks in a steady voice. Outside, air currents coax in the first rains of the season. A nurse nods in agreement and turns their listening inward.

"And if the heart speaks — Listen.
And if the heart listens, you may speak."

The earth also calls us

Tomb

We share

this

Promise

Otur

                                        where you are
                                        Otur

as in

                                        to be seated

to live well,   to gather
to speak,   to be spoken
to/of
sit   certain
/to nourish/selves/to rest/and Saturday through/
             in this place
as in
together
             and see
             there
gaze
upon

                                             your children
this is
    what you   can   know of
                                             peace

i.
I am not afraid of the four-legged creatures that approach through
the day. Although I might be tempted to escort them

through the curtain of my mouth, they remain as guests. Other times
they osmose through the distanced membranes and demand more than feasting.

Their yellow teeth paint into lanes of a winding road that leads away from home,
and the intoxication of the asphalt is a fine fuel that spools hereditary spines.

ii.

My mother's Jeep Liberty, which has travailed thousands of miles
                through New Mexico roads
and has braved many New Orleans potholes, has finally revived in the

cold wet of the Pacific Northwest.
Its growling engine and prancing movements balance across

the tremendous girth of four agile snow tires.
When I am driving, I think of all the miles traversed,

and the gauge on the dashboard counts them back to me,
one mile for every missed hunt.

iii.

The wolf is lucid with ember eyes, matted hair, the night—
lean with hunger and purpose.

She stalks my heat in the crumbling ionosphere of
the holocene tree, the last standing sentinel of the burnt enclave.

She perceives that I mean no harm
to the cub that skirts to my right, playing with a brittle bone

between his paws. His white teeth, new and urgent, scrape the sky.
I wander in the elegy of the tree,

unaware of this instinct that must exact its boundaries,
regardless of intention.

She approaches by my left flank and presses me down.
I feel her breath in my ear, the saliva, thick with the primal covenant.

iv.
Amygdala unpetals,
a voice plumes
to the surface——

burns deeply down into the armature
of each cell——

this rhythmic force,
mother——

v.

All other motions of confusion
are elementary languages in the belly
of an insatiable star trembling into storied ash.

vi.

Beneath the vibration of the dream engine,
I sense a fine silt of grief

across the skin of this earth,
my every padded foothold,

my every urge to bite against redemption
for that which I transformed.

Pair of
hands

        mounding

ashes

the   ashes

still lit

        embers

Gris la casa   perfumada   de trueno   cerrado
Donde   habitan   mil rencores   pulidos.
Murmuran   impacientes sobre   las primeras tejadas
    De   la   imprudente   noche.
No esperan   nada ya   de ti.
Silencio   sus ojos en nudos de   luz
    Apriétense   y apréstense.
    Seca   y ceñida   de cascabel   la boca
El bosque   sigue su   marcha.
No   (con)sigas para   atrás.
El altar   de implícita sal   y   ordenanzas de   calavera
No espera.   No devuelve la espuma   de la creación.

Disuelva   diosa hembra   purgada,
Luego   el penúltimo   relámpago
    En el tinto   de
Su propia pluma.
Ahí   nos deja
En esta   ceremonia despejada
    Para los que no escuchan
    La voz   del   grillo   invertido:
Yo digo:
    Perdón.
Yo pido:
      La barranca
      De gracia.
Y
   Brinca

In the floating world	our words suspend beyond
si	lence
Rain falls behind	telegraphed lines
embattled	with the prism
listens	toward
any motion of grace	Green crickets slip their
twigged legs along	the seams of our attention
wide	ning
the solid	the unsolid
the vision in	revealing through
parting	overhead
Blue star	braids
its	arms
into the end	less of its blue
Someone speaks of a wolf	calling words fall to the floor
And	
I	limn
this endless	perpendicular
where all worlds	that are no
worlds	intercalate

PART 3

THE CALL

Sunlight shifts thoughts along the corner of this
barren table. Where there is no food,
you are sustained. Where there is no water to drink,
rain falls in full trails. Where there is shadow,
color breaks the heart open, gently
at first, then further for forage.

worry not
how others pronounce

/the call

yours alone

to answer/

1.

The path winding up from the parking lot

    where routine disperses into sunbaked silence,

        rubber pooling beneath the tired vehicles

            and loose ends of conversations dangling out in the breeze,

                tethered to their circumstances.

        From there up we go. Fumbling over stones and scree

            toward the clerestory of

      pine and bough, twigs caught in an empty

clear space, the logs fallen. I walked there holding

   you while the

      way was too steep

                for you to gaze and

wonder and not fall. I thought of

      the water and the bread of our lives, wrapped softly in

        the canvas of my chest,

          plotting out when you might

        need to drink and eat of it.

      I heard the sound

   of dogs barking when we reached the top.

                    You squealed out to be set free.

2.

Legs cycling faster until there were four, six, sixteen

and twenty-one miles between us and yet I can

see your hair in the vivid green frost of the understory.

Here, foal cross streams as wide as prairies

and deep as the touch of your hand. How far we came,

stopping to eat

or drink cool waters when the agile and

impatient spring lodged its spacious hull in our throats.

You laughed as I called out for you to come,

dancing across the roots, eyes swimming

with steam and melodies that I can

hear you singing to the rhythm of new words.

You begin and I repeat and will

repeat again while we sort these all out:

songs precarious and fragile still—

like river stones, the gray and flat or red and round.

Run through with delight, tears, at times

frustration. We celebrate when we find the

blue, the green. The part where I recognize

and you affirm, drawing from our alluvial inheritance—

the perfect one that fits your palm,

my palm. We admire and exchange what we find,

before we set it all aside for a further time,

along the way.

Petals hydrolyze the

1:48 pm sun,

green or sure somehow

its movement, traces along

the wandering roots of an apple tree,

dresses the small garden in

fluid architecture.

An exhilarated wheelbarrow tips to its side,

exhales a glory of mottled

weeds, and

yellowjackets exhume

the channels of a forgotten

vole maze.

Heavy and aching

fruits reach groundward,

a drifting clause

longs

for release, snaps

where

thin

and this——

the grafted branch of an afternoon,

searching for a way

beyond

the limbs/the tongue,

appendix announcing memory,

the way it struggles

to root storms,

wanes when the land starves.

Where

in the harsh angle

of thirsting root

to supple stem

does the body

lean to/soften against

as to the shaded ground

the yellowjackets, their patient bite

or other stars,

their bodies furred with fresh foxglove pollen,

swaying color into shape, the rain

plummeting to its depth,

for ripen in skull a

constancy

of manifold moons,

girdling the canes of

viscid light.

The world lay strewn in pieces across the kitchen floor.

No harm shall save, no harm shall break.

Walking amidst fruit trees,

the newness

rivers

her open.

In this place that is no place but place, no time but time

where all words instill understanding

and hold the world steady after all verses ending—

they watch from the tree as the children play

in the garden, by the river . . .

What was the question your heart was asking?

-Who watches from the orchard?
-Who wanders by the river?

All who attend the silence
understand.

Y qué preguntaba tú corazón?

-Quién mira desde el frutal?
-Quién pasea por la orilla del riachuelo?

Quienes atienden el silencio
comprenden.

Those who recalled what happened looked
        row ahead   without veil
their faces   without shroud
four-chambered and steady

Someone spoke with no need for reply

                                            Flow

          it travels from   far curve of

                                            planet

How it scoops the gleaming mosaic of rivers
and gathers the bird-rippled indigo of dawn
the clean liquid prism of fish   *how it*
echoed the first, flaming candle
and lovingly enumerated the sharp, wet leaves
of the pomegranate tree and

                                    followed itself forth

through oceans and oceans
torrents upon placid

                                    to this place

these words

And suddenly, the mind ceases its clatter

The body leaves its moment for the
first direction,

bends below its own horizon

Along the pleural boundaries
of memory, a radicle

urging. Thick and damp the silver

rains where first thought /im/
planted

the full and tough kernel
its sweet starch
thickly milking
through miles of fur. Now

pluck some tender petals and
bundle
together

the forest that leads out of this forest.

Grains of wind blow forward the rhizomes.
Expansion sews,
even as it thins illumination
in passing.

A cupola appears overhead, ripening—

I was afraid

                              -she admits

de algo parecido a la palabra for memory

          el anochecer abre sus alas en un arco de alambre morado

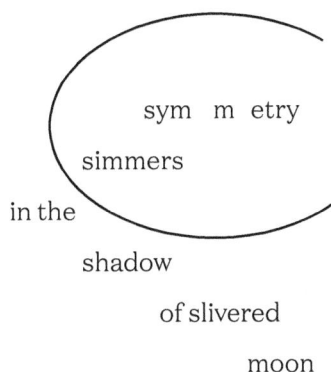

sym m etry

simmers

in the

shadow

of slivered

moon

Third House seems an ordinary place on a busy suburban street
beset by garbage cans and ponds of oil lining the pockets of an early
hour, the gesture of habitat expending itself into the guttural rip of the traffic
on a nearby overpass.

The porch is a red-tailed falcon, its obsidian talons point north in direction
of an E-sharp chord of wind. It picks at the waspy carcass of a yellow sky.
Clouds spawn overhead and scuttle towards the mountain cradle, their breath
shallow and short.

An insipid rhododendron, aching for iron, traces into a draping ascent
and serrates the sturdy movements of the hellebore fang.

We enter the cadmium house and gather in the dark living room,
weary and dilapidated. Our organs wilted and waxen with the
need for sleep and sleep.

Food is prepared for us, and we learn to feed each other in
a percussive silence of grains. It is in the nature of us,
this need for ritual. Even if we are grieving, even if we are starving.

When, after a century, I open my left eye to speak, I tell of how I have died in the
First House and the Second, and how *bir süre sonra*, I crossed a chasm of
       chaos. I want
the others to know the contours of my story. Their attention gathers
into dense folds and we merge over the kitchen table,

our heads bowed like light poles,
even as the First and Second Houses shudder, shake
and empty.

A patient curtain of yarrow embraces the fallen buildings. The cold blue
        of their fences
pale as corpses as they descend into the black compost.
A swarm of damselflies erupts from the tattered graves and

we await the
dull blade of the winter sun
to blunt and crack these dreams of survival.

There will be no need for explanation because we learned
how to hour, how to move through this liminal procession in
an offering of images:

ours will be barely ripened tomatoes from a dormant garden,
hard and stringent juice leaking with each bite
and enough thick blankets to keep everyone warm on those

cold nights, purloined from
the mouths of those who would
eat the world entero.

PART 4

SICAK AYETLER

Each day

a new sun awakens

arrives

in a stream of photons

that

trickle

warmly

down

the arm

and into

each verse.

That row we watch,

that part in the garden that is ready

to seed

        to quark

how each small change,

the swelling, the dry,

the thinning, and the falling

        forever

the lap of the earth

which part is needed for saving, for the

clouded, the

        gravity

the contours that friction it, with

each word, each small

act of

        almanac——

they flow from fallow

into the rill of these songs

where we once played.

And what are you afraid of?

     the soul does not need to answer

          the answer knows itself too well

              to have need of speech

into the blue forever

     and the gathering of clouds that

          were sent today——

a locution of atmospheres,

     exhaling the patient ash

          of silence

the clouds are curious again

as they lay their paths across

the folding crease of radiance

into darkness.

how they admire everything,

the way the colors resolve

into quiet winds

the russet tapestries

of furred autumns,

bark bracing up the depths

in the slow gravitational

lumber below.

they stare straight

into the fact

of the ocean, slipping

praise from their heavy tongues

each time

a phytoplankton blush emerges

into bluegreen dreaming.

do they imagine the fragile reach

of life's transparent filaments,

the feathered girth of shadows,

or the lavender ease

with which the cliffs open for each dawning,

each eon of river,

woven into the warp of

their plunging depths.

do the clouds

long to descend and catch

the fat moon on their shoulders,

or feed her immense beams

into concentrated pools,

luscious drippings in the pan of

these wide, stark meadows. will they

taste the dense and marrowed

bite of being

as they reach their arms down to

turn piled sand in their palms

over and over so tender

as if they were kneading

warm dough.

or do they only wish to break

themselves

on each tiny grain of

ground, to hear

their own voices

split cold into soil,

where they will echo

through this

root urge to

become

sky again.

i.   Walking beneath the maple tree

ii.   Tree is young yet, not much more than a sapling

iii.   This is where the words arrived in my small hands

The fifth petal of the evening opens——

the sound of   dice,

those kinds of talks   *Things are alright...*

Home waiting out there in the world.

Somewhere in the coming days, the laughter

of children, onions frying, a half-completed puzzle.

The novel tipped behind the couch

mouthfuls of chips while cleaning the floors

with lavender-scented chemicals in a house

where a man once shot his wife.

There are still stories that fill the mouths with peace,

even if the daily reality

breaks the body by intervals. In the mornings I open

the windows to let fresh air find me. I call a friend.

We talk and wonder aloud about our parents,

how they raised us, what lexicons they

designed, and what they could not sustain.

We were daughters, once, after all.

And how to manage this humanity?

I give this work to a galaxy of

prayers

plucked from the branch of September's latest harvest.

When I have energy,

I make apple sauce, apple butter.

A pressure cooker quickens the work. I remove

the brown spots where the worms have burrowed.

I chop and slice, and chop and slice.

And I remember the

icy, delicate flowers that the apples once were,

the slow way their swelling bodies filled

a tight, summer heat. How

their pink and yellow gradients rounded out the days, or

how the night alighted—

a fresh peel on my tongue.

In the recesses of a cloud quickly shifting
there is a sentience, swallow-tailed and gliding,
though the fragrance of a moment
cannot conceal the waning trajectory
taken to find this place.

      (You capture meaning by gestures,

      shallow perhaps

      and what will sustain you once the cold parallel

      evaporates?)

No matter the unknown course of tomorrow, or the following
day, fresh words will comfort,
though they be the same words. They
knit into the crescent of heliosphere beneath
which a gaze suspends
its

            first elevation

(and you
remembered

      the answer was yours to give

in
the
axis
of exhale)

This fire is pronounced in a hope for blue. Wonders whether it is the first somatic sacrifice and dances to the warmth of the thought. There is a rain falling across a pure and perfect crust of snow. The way the slush and melt of it into mud. Radio waves are themselves cousins of heat. They make their way out to Jupiter, to the abandoned sweetness of Pluto. Even this place has its own knowledge of the warmth of seasons, though they be too long for reckoning. Someone's hearing is dilating in the dark branches of a fruit tree. This, too, is a warmth. No need for images, just the script. It moves mouths and molecules, this we know. And movement, in any context, warms. Time, the scientists tell us—also a function of heat. Water doesn't know what it means to oblige. It seeks the cracks and yields shoreline. This entropy, also warm. And so it is that earnest green shoots will raise their heads in the gasket of another dawn. The clouds will speckle and crack. The air in this hemisphere is shorn and quartite. A heavy architrave warms that seasoned desire, even as it expands the angles between discrete bodies. As everything descends into the coldest nadir, a swerving atom may melt the helium eye when least expected. Then, is it too simple of me when I say—I want to do good things in this world.

The body felt it was a table for fur and other minute supplements both mineral and animal in the cold climate that arrived in tatters, hungry and ready to set its teeth into anything. There beside the body sat the stone, perhaps flint, or chert, rather. It paced the nanoseconds in wait for the body to take it into itself again as body. To chip away at the sunrise one more time. How strong and mighty a hand that touched itself to this task, hard like a plank of cedar, or a slicing feather. Bent to nothing but the damp hope of body.

The body cut itself with itself. Something came, cold and clear like ruin. Then the body sent packages, gifts of apology for what it had done in that moment of the body. The offerings arrived quickly, all bound together and clotted up with glue and platelets, as if that were to suffice for urgency. For days, the body didn't cry about what it had done. Two weeks later the festering body sang out in the dark for a hot iron, a pinch of salt and a steel moon in which to sink itself in afterward. The body answered, and it arrived there both cold and shallow.

The body set about to knit another body from within. It started with small goals: milestones with which to congratulate itself along the way. Research, an important thing for the body. To measure itself against the body's idea of growth and development. This was the inevitable path to new body becoming. Which was nothing less than good ground.

The body first opened all the valves along this terrain, one course of body and then another. This effected a great spill of accelerant over everything, the body and itself. A spark of something, perhaps attention, caught the edge of the body and zipped the chert into a feasting yellow flame. This fire warmed the body nicely. The body had been so cold.

The body at last latched itself onto the warmth, just as it had hoped to, but had never imagined it would do in that lifetime. From that moment on, the body set about pulling away its precious furs. One follicle for every ice age.

PART 5

AFTER ALL VERSES ENDING

"The mountains loom and recede. And
Below, the umber plain is a pitted hide"
—N. Scott Momaday, "La Tierra del Encanto"

Breath scatters into echo on the eastern flanks of the caldera.
A lingering fire sharpens its long tooth with ponderosa pine,
and spindly aspens relinquish gold coins unto it for my ransom.

I follow the path that traces towards the naked sky
muscling hard through the lichened basalt and pumice
to the place that time has sculpted on the cerulean cliff.

High on the back of the little bird, something watches
across the vast plain that imagines itself into golden feathers—
discrete its obsidian beak cleaving into hard horizons here.

I cup my hands towards the east. I wonder what I mean when I
say to the tough and certain wind: *I am longing...*
as a pair of tumbleweeds stiffen and roll past my legs.

The dogs carve their paws into the soft earth, a vein
of Cenozoic tuff exposed beneath clouds of powdery dust. They rush
          towards me
and then disappear into the chamisa.

Once, when I was a child, I huddled down out here

between the giant boulders

for hours, matching my shaking breath to the rhythm of the roiling gusts.

Longing is a praise that ruptures, devours.

After a while. the dogs return with a dead

 baby rabbit, its neck broken, eyes glassing.

I place its body in a small hole in the ground and begin the descent.

Longing is a burial ritual for all the hours.

A vanquished sun empties out

across the opening expanse. The umber hide fades along the wide curve,

caught in its instinct for gravity below.

A spider untangles   its flame

from

thick and   sweet vein——

I had given up.

No radio waves or get-well cards

from seven continents.

No seashells, no shelter, no face.

Then,

I heard words being spoken

I willed them to unfasten for me.

They asked me to gather my implements

and open white flame.

For, as small as that first aperture appeared, it was.

Among all things of color and motion,

it was   most pure.

The call hears me more clearly
than I can hear it.

Consider one rainbow, the rain supine.

The raised edge of holly branch. Scarlet slice.

Young maple drinks deeply into its colored throat

spirals its boughs.

Second rainbow   carves sacrifice

as the words   arrive

on their own   feet.

This is the place where   ***lullabies are born***
patterning themselves
in turquoise and   ***corals***
along the currents
                                     of memory

Every day must be
a chance to breathe
the intricacy
of oxygen,
the scent of the seas.
Its endless darkening.
Its three long inhales.

And it was said
that
each new wave
calls   ***in***

          the   ***language of***
                         of our being

Everything may happen in this season—

Even that which will be forgotten.

All seek their place
in compassion.

It is nighttime. Electrons bleed out into inky, indigo swathes.
Patterns emerge amidst the stippled surfaces of the ceiling tiles;
at times they resolve into familiar faces, at other times
they dissolve into endless script.
Heavy pillars of concrete steady
the sound of rain falling on the metal roof.
An unhurried river reaches its arms into felsic crevice,
its warm breathing sculpting dreams to be set loose upon the earth
and the rain aligns.
Pathways between the crease of gray matter and burnished clouds are
the crossing of index over thumb, the whorls on each fingertip, or
the questions that pupate and calcify across generations.
These were the years that were not an obligation.
A small cylinder of white silver
placed beneath the pilgrimage of moons to signal junction.
Each tectonic movement of hands smoothing away the rough textures
         of routine.
Hours brushing away a generous snow that has landed across the

wide mouth of the caldera in higher altitudes. A wolf
stalking a deer in the thicket of young aspen, its heart pumping.
Pupils dilate. The wind swallows the scent of hunger
and crosses the divide.
All that remains is pattern, is beauty.
Shells stacked together,
River stones that anchor the arroyo
and stories that spawn centuries with each footfall.
This must be more than gesture—to tide further into
the incomprehensible dome arranging, constantly arranging.

A four-chambered heart can blossom

into   l

The monument weighs heavily.

A   lodestar,

meteorite.

Each   wavelength

of   instruction

blue with   intent.

We have carried   these words

in   our hearts

and spoken with them so many times,

not even we knew what we were saying.

The heart opens itself in battle.

The silhouette, it shifts.

A desert, it quiets.

A revelation to the sea, it subducts.

A return to the East, it surfaces.

To the East   it voice.

To the East   it ask

this star and

surrender

into the last row

Bir sure sonra   *bile yoktu*

       (hiçbir şey yoktu).

Sonra ağaçta   *oturdu*

       ve nehir kenarında bahçede

       oynuyordu çocuklar.

Not even a verse after

       (there was nothing).

Then,

       they were sitting in the tree

and watched

the children playing in the garden,
by the river.

NOTE ON LANGUAGE

Three languages appear in this book. While the poems are predominately in English, Spanish and Turkish are also interwoven throughout. Although English is my first language, I write frequently in Spanish, having learned while growing up in New Mexico and later in more depth while living in Latin America. My partner is from Turkey, and we spend ample time there with family, where I am also learning Turkish.

The final poem, "10/1.1 Bir sıra sonra," was the first poem that came to me and formed the basis of this collection. This poem was written after a period of reading Turkish children's stories to my son, where the common phrase *bir süre sonra*, meaning "a little while later", appeared often. I enjoyed the interplay between the words *sıra* (row, line, place, or queue), *süre* (time, period, or duration), and *sure* (surah, from Arabic, meaning a chapter from the Qu'ran). Although the meanings are markedly different, this book explores the poetic possibilities of viewing these words almost as homologs.

Many of the non-English language sections have direct translations while others do not. The poem, "9/27.8 Otur," for instance, provides a creative interpretation of the Turkish verb, *oturmak* meaning "to sit" (*otur* being the imperative mood). In Turkish, the word has many implications: When you ask someone where they live, you do not use the verb "to live," but rather ask "where do you all sit?" *Oturmak* in Turkish implies living, enjoyment, time spent with loved ones, drinking tea, perhaps in a garden or other comfortable settings, and may have historical connotations. It is interesting to me particularly because for much of history, Turkish tribes were nomadic; it was not until the occupation of Anatolia that various dynasties, particularly the Ottomans, began to adopt various cultural and literary practices of their Persian and Arab neighbors—including poetry and the courtly lifestyle. *Oturmak* is thus a richly layered concept and could perhaps be called a philosophy of life that is difficult to translate directly to English. For the collection, *oturmak* has a more personal meaning as well, as the speaker reflects on what is essential or elemental in their life as they seek a new mode of being in the world.

The presence of Spanish in this book is more fragmented or textural and is intended to evoke memories of place and mood. One of the Spanish language poems does not include a translation in the book, "9/28.2 And a cricket jumps." This poem is conceived of as an evocation of various forms of sacrificial acts ending in a gesture towards forgiveness that is embodied in the image of a leap (*brinca*). According to Sebastián de Covarrubias in *Tesoro de la lengua castellana o española* published in 1611, *brincar* (the infinitive) bears similarities to the movements of dancers or goats jumping from rock to rock. He also makes mention of its relationship to the word *brinco*, meaning a small jewel suspended from a headdress (folio 105v.) Other etymologists posit that *brinca* derives from the Latin *vinculum*, meaning chain, link, or fastening—implying perhaps that while there is sense of being unmoored or unbound, one may also exist as or share in a field of attachment or connection. *Brinca* is thus not a permanent state of suspension but rather necessarily implies the essential force that unites a subject with another subject(s) or object(s), perhaps the most explicit reference being the gravity that balances us in relation to the earth. As a layered interpretation, the implied linkage might also refer to the birth chord. There are other forces that hold us steady or provide us with a source of faith, whether they be physical or non-physical beings, texts, dreams, or ideas. This *brinca* thus may also relate to the "leap" of faith that has been an important part of my personal process while writing these poems. I felt immersed in the intuitive experience that particular words and sounds elicited. They seemed to take me into another realm where my routine mental habits dissipated, and new visions and songs took form. As an incantation, the integrity of the language/orality of the text figures as elemental with regards to meaning and intention.

The overarching hope is that the experience of moving through texts in multiple languages will reflect the nebulous sensation of writing and experiencing poetry, where it is not always clear where or why the words originate in the way that they do. This movement dislocates our perceptions and destabilizes expectations. Even when speaking or reading in one's native language(s), the layers of meaning and relational implications embedded often escape awareness. This effect is even more evident when reading and hearing languages with which one may be unfamiliar. In language, we can lose our essential sense of self only to rediscover new ways of knowing, not knowing, understanding, searching, and feeling. The use of multiple languages thus creates communicative potential and opens our connection to larger systems of thoughts, beliefs, and ways of being that interweave all life—plant, animal, and mineral. Languages also carry with them a ritual genealogy that encompasses the registers of sensory impressions, relationships, histories, and earth memory. These poems invite the reader to participate in the liminal spaces where poetry emerges and enables language to become conscious of itself through the transformative power of loss and healing that mark our shared human existence.

ACKNOWLEDGMENTS

Many thanks to the other members of the First Matter Press 2022 cohort for providing invaluable feedback, camaraderie, laughter, and insight as we prepared our manuscripts for publication: ahuva s. zaslavsky, Xylophone Mykland, Riley Danvers, and Hailey Spencer. I also want to thank my lead editors, Caroline Reul and Lauren Paredes, who helped me to refine and reflect on the text with patience and grace. Many appreciations to Ash Good, for their constant support, professionalism, and expertise throughout this journey. I feel incredibly grateful to Rachel Mulder for the beautiful artwork that graces the cover of this book. So much gratitude to Natalie Garyet and Emily Moon for their editing and insightful presence at our workshops. It has been a remarkable experience to share in the presence of such wonderful poets, artists, and lovely humans. I also thank my partner, Afşın, for supporting me in pursuing this project and for providing insight into the Turkish language. And to my beautiful son, Çağrı, for accompanying me through workshops and editing sessions. You inspire me, and I am so proud of you. To New Mexico, for feeding me with imagination, health, stories, and happiness. The area in which I grew up includes the traditional homelands of the Jemez (Walatowa), San Ildefonso (Po-Wo-Geh Owingeh), and Santa Clara (Ka'p'oe'Owingeh) Puebloan peoples and their ancestors. Many of the places referenced in the poems were forcibly taken from Indigenous peoples through various stages of settler-colonization that continue through the present and with which my own story is enmeshed. I acknowledge that these poems were written on the unceded homelands of the Coast Salish people, specifically the Squaxin Island and Nisqually peoples. I want to thank these lands and those who have cared for them for cloaking us in gentle rains and generous forests. To Ayvalık—to the Aegean Sea, to shorelines, dry winds, the hourglass elegance of the tea glass, street cats, and sunsets. To my mother—for teaching me the importance of inner creativity. Her memory continues to guide me in every aspect of life. To my father and brother, remembrances of the trails, geological appreciations, and shared histories. To the spirits of Madison and Jackson, my faithful companions. To all the black holes in the universe, for keeping mystery alive.

SONYA WOHLETZ was born as a bat in a cave in New Mexico territory. Having since transformed into a human, she now enjoys the use of opposable thumbs to write, paint, cook, and make glorious messes. Her work has appeared in *Latin American Literary Review*, *Revolute*, and *Roanoke Review*, among others.

FIRSTMATTERPRESS
Portland, Ore.

First Matter Press is a collective press in Portland, Oregon, founded in 2018 to dissolve publication barriers for first-time publishing poets and genre-expanding writers. Our annual releases center community and craft by inviting authors into a creative cohort where they crystallize manuscripts in dialogue with editors and fellow writers and collaborate with featured artists on original cover art.

We are a 501(c)(3) non-profit organization and our authors maintain 100% copyrights and sales royalties of published work. Find our titles at IndieBound.org, Powells.com, BN.com and other major bookseller websites.

2022
FEATURED COVER ARTIST RACHEL MULDER

BETWEEN THESE BORDERS WANDERS A GOLEM
ahuva s. zaslavsky

EVEN THE AIR, TOO HEAVY
riley danvers

ONE ROW AFTER / BIR SIRA SONRA
sonya wohletz

SOMEONE I CAN HOLD GENTLY
xylophone mykland

STORIES FOR WHEN THE WOLVES ARRIVE
hailey spencer

FIRSTMATTERPRESS.ORG

2021
FEATURED COVER ARTIST ALEKSANDRA APOCALISSE

CONSIDER THE BODY, WINGED
jessica e. pierce

ROUTES BETWEEN RAINDROPS
dan wiencek

THE GROWTH LINES
gabby hancher

2020
FEATURED COVER ARTIST SARA SWOBODA

BODY UNTIL LIGHT
k.m. lighthouse

IT'S JUST YOU & ME, MISS MOON
emily moon

LOVERS AND OTHER STILL CREATURES
eitan codish

2019
FEATURED COVER ARTIST HELLSEA

OTHERWISE, MAGIC
lauren paredes

THE NIGHT SKY IS A PLACE WHERE THINGS GET LOST
andrew chenevert

TIME COUNTS BACKWARD FROM INFINITY
k.m. lighthouse

WE ARE NOT READY FOR WHAT WE ARE
ash good

2018
FEATURED COVER ARTIST HOLGER LIPPMANN

SOUNDS IN MY MÖBIUS MIND
ash good

YOU ARE AN AMBIGUOUS PRONOUN
k.m. lighthouse

www.ingramcontent.com/pod-product-compliance
Lightning Source LLC
Chambersburg PA
CBHW051635120626
46551CB00014B/2089

* 9 7 8 1 9 5 8 6 0 0 0 4 7 *